25 LESSONS
WHAT WE LEARNED FROM OPRAH

Nancy Mehagian & Judith A. Proffer

Copyright 2011 by Nancy Mehagian,
Judith A. Proffer and Huqua Press
All rights reserved.

ISBN 978-0-9838120-0-5

First published in 2011 by Huqua Press.
A division of Magpye Media/Morling Manor Corp.
Los Angeles, California

Cover design by Hugh Syme.

Interior Design by Integrative Ink.

No part of this book may be reproduced or transmitted in any form by any means without permission from the author or publisher.

Any views, opinions, writings or other content of this book expressed in any manner including what has been learned from watching twenty-five years of the Oprah Winfrey Show are solely those of the authors and do not represent those of Oprah Winfrey, Harpo Productions or anyone associated with Oprah Winfrey or her entities, in any manner whatsoever. Nothing in this book should be construed as emanating from Oprah Winfrey or Harpo Productions.

A portion of the proceeds from the sale of this book will assist arts and education.

For everyone of us that succeeds, it's because there's somebody to show you the way out. The light doesn't always necessarily have to be in your family; for me it was teachers and school.

- Oprah Winfrey

For Jessica, David, Victoria and Brianna.
Even when life startles, there is love and there is light.

Contents

INTRODUCTION ix

LESSON 1 ~ LOOK FOR THE LESSON 1

LESSON 2 ~ SEEK RENEWAL IN NATURE 5

LESSON 3 ~ ATTRACT A FORMIDABLE AND
               FOREVER SIDEKICK 9

LESSON 4 ~ READ OFTEN 13

LESSON 5 ~ OWN YOURSELF 17

LESSON 6 ~ INTENTION.......................................21

LESSON 7 ~ LOVE IS IN THE DETAILS 25

LESSON 8 ~ WHEN YOU KNOW BETTER
               YOU DO BETTER 29

LESSON 9 ~ TAKE RISKS 33

LESSON 10 ~ GIVE FREELY, RECEIVE GRACIOUSLY 37

LESSON 11 ~ AGE GRATEFULLY 41

LESSON 12 ~ EMBRACE A SPIRITUAL QUEST 45

LESSON 13 ~ UNDERSTAND KARMIC LAW 49

LESSON 14 ~ CREATE JOY AND LAUGH OFTEN...............53

LESSON 15 ~ I NEVER THOUGHT OF IT
                THAT WAY BEFORE 57

LESSON 16 ~ DON'T LET MOMENTS DEFINE YOU,
                LET THEM DIVINE YOU 61

LESSON 17 ~ ASK THE TOUGH QUESTIONS 65

LESSON 18 ~ CULTIVATE FORGIVENESS 69

LESSON 19 ~ FIND YOUR CALLING 73

LESSON 20 ~ DO WHAT YOU LOVE 77

LESSON 21 ~ BE A STUDENT FOR LIFE 81

LESSON 22 ~ CREATE A VISION BOARD 87

LESSON 23 ~ BE OF SERVICE 91

LESSON 24 ~ NOURISH AND NURTURE YOURSELF 95

LESSON 25 ~ ENDINGS AREN'T ENDINGS;
THEY'RE BEGINNINGS IN DIFFERENT
SUITS OF CLOTHING 99

ACKNOWLEDGEMENTS 105

INTRODUCTION

I was late arriving to the Oprah party. Between work, travel, and a disinterest in daytime television I could count on two hands the number of Oprah shows I had seen over the years—until her 25th season. Her pull-out-all-the stops extravaganza of reunions, now or never topics, now or never guests and great big teaching moments was a whirlwind of entertainment and enlightenment.

A week or two into this final year my friend Nancy raved to me about a particularly compelling Oprah episode and said, "You really should record this season. It's going to be so good." So this was the understanding—I set my DVR to record every show and Nancy would tell me which ones I absolutely could not miss. Beneath the veneer of famous faces I was struck by the lessons that were the cornerstone of each show. Some lessons were gentle whispers, some were like a hammer to the head; but lessons they were, each and every offering.

I noted that Oprah used her platform to do some of the things I have used my own (albeit *significantly* smaller) media platform to do— illuminate, inspire and educate. I witnessed Oprah the teacher at work. I enjoyed the guests who were there to entertain but were also there to inform. I got it.

In April 2011, a month before Oprah took her leave from her weekday perch, my husband was mulling over a complex business decision.

"Ah," I said to him, "if you attended Oprah University you wouldn't be this perplexed."

The Oprah show the day before had shed light on something that I sort of knew, having to do with intention. I wed my own understanding with Oprah's spin on spiritual law to ease his burden about this particular quandary.

The next day while hiking in the mountains near my San Fernando Valley home the idea for this book came to me like a thunderbolt. So many of the lessons I saw come to life on Oprah's show are things I have learned from various teachers, healers, friends and experts over the past two and a half decades of living in Los Angeles. I have learned by living and taking risks and making mistakes and by surrounding myself with wisdom and grace. And I learned that just because we amass life-altering lessons along the way, it's a blessing to have this information punctuated, often when we need it most. Ever the student. Ever evolving.

I approached Nancy to join me on this project. In encouraging me to revel in all this final season had to offer, she in fact was offering me a refresher course in key elements of Enlightened Living 101. Together we decided to share some personal stories to showcase how we have put this knowledge into action over the years.

This book is an homage to the top twenty-five lessons we believe Oprah viewers, both the new and the devout, can connect with. Read these lessons and you'll enjoy a refresher course in some of media's greatest teachings. *Own* these twenty-five lessons and you'll live in authenticity, abundance, clarity and joy.

~ Judith A. Proffer

When I think of Oprah the word "integrity" comes to mind. That's what touches me so deeply about this beloved media figure—her honesty. If everyone could be as honest as Oprah, what a world this would be. So when Judy came to me with her idea for this book, my first thought was, "What would Oprah think about it?" Then I thought, as long as it's honest and from the heart, it might earn her stamp of approval. Oprah has touched so many people in so many different ways. I am delighted to have the opportunity to share my own feelings about her as well as pass on some key lessons she has shared with us over the years.

As a massage therapist I had the privilege of working on Oprah a couple of times and it was an absolute pleasure. I loved her complete lack of pretense. Being in her presence was like meeting up with someone I've known for a long time. One of my favorite stories about her has come from Stedman Graham, Oprah's partner of many years, who just can't get over the fact that she takes her own lunch to work every day. Hearing that has warmed my heart even more.

I never saw Oprah shine more brightly than she did by the final shows of Season 25. There was something about her that broadcast an unmistakable sense of levity. She carried so much responsibility—and carried it so well—for those 25 years. I was thrilled that she was preparing to take some time and space just for herself.

I am eternally grateful for all of Oprah's good works and for the myriad ways in which she has used her life for the benefit of others. What an inspiration she has been for people everywhere. She has demonstrated over and over again what one person, with a heart as wide as the world, can accomplish. In the midst of all the craziness out there we are so fortunate to have had Oprah—a constant reminder of balance, generosity and grace.

~ Nancy Mehagian

LESSON 1

LOOK FOR THE LESSON

"The sages do not consider that making no mistakes is a blessing. They believe rather that the great virtue of man lies in his ability to correct his mistakes and continually make a new man of himself."
~ Wang Yang Ming

Oprah has often said that had she not followed the media path that beckoned her she would have become a teacher. For the millions who attended "Oprah University" every day, we know that in actuality she didn't forgo a teaching career. She *is* America's teacher.

As the professor of possibilities, she dared us to hitch a ride for the journey of a lifetime. Oprah's classroom was a studio with the greatest show and tell on earth and her students were rapt. Her chalkboard was our soul where she left an indelible imprint.

She guided us toward reading and eating and viewing and thinking and moving and reveling and being. And one of the greatest lessons we cull from twenty-five years is a not so gentle reminder to look for the lesson.

We learned that every obstacle is in fact a lesson—a gateway to our truth. Each hardship, each "no," each road block, each frustrating or unexplainable or even awkward event is intended to illuminate and educate—to guide us onto the right path or to inspire us to explore a new action or way of thinking.

Above all Oprah has taught us that looking for the lesson is about learning to dialogue with our inner self or a higher power. Friends and family may gently guide us with insight and perspective on any given matter but the lesson is only truly learned when we have that "aha" moment that connects our dots, practically and spiritually.

> ***When we look for the lesson and find it within, only then do we get a "passing grade" and move on to the next level of emotional and spiritual evolution.***

Huka, my fawn pug, was just three years old. My fur child with chocolate pudding eyes is a mirthful and loving spirit. She is my sweet and silly sidekick. One of the great loves of my life.

She was due for her vaccines. On the way to the vet, my head rattled with doubt and fear. "Is it really okay for duplicate vaccines to be administered at once? Is that too much for my fourteen-pound pup? Should I have done more research?" My veterinarian had assured me two weeks earlier that it's common practice and is less stressful and less invasive for the animal when you "get it over with." As I handed my precious bundle to the vet technician, I echoed the discontent rumbling in my stomach: "Is it protocol for her to have more than one vaccination at once?"

"We do it all the time," was the comforting reply.

Fifteen minutes later a sprightly and sassy Huka was squirming in my embrace. She even tossed a little growl the way of the vet tech as we exited the office. I exhaled. All was good.

Ten minutes into our drive home things went horribly wrong. Huka began to vomit and struggled to maintain consciousness. I pleaded with her to hold on and somehow safely navigated the drive back to the vet. The waiting room was filled with people, cats, dogs and frustration. The office was behind schedule and an emergency meant all of those waiting would wait even longer. Their scowls gave way to compassion when they saw me awash in fear and vomit. Three veterinarians struggled to save her. And they did.

The lessons were large. Since that averted tragedy I have never let the voice inside me remain quiet. I have *learned to trust my instincts. I also took an online vet technician course to be more aware and involved in my dogs' health care. I learned that community appears in the most surprising of places. The eight or so people in the waiting room that day became my family and Huka's cheerleaders for those two harrowing hours. They stayed with me and held my hand until my husband arrived. Their compassion was extraordinary and something I will long remember.*

Two years later my husband Spencer and I were leashing up Huka and our male pug Quincy for a twilight walk. As I slipped the harness over Quincy's head intuition told me to abort the walk. I told Spencer that instead of a stroll I just wanted to take them out quickly in the backyard. Neighbors told me the next morning that they had seen two coyotes trolling the neighborhood, brazenly walking down our street at the very time we were about to walk the pups. My peace of mind and their well being both remained intact as a direct result of heeding my inner voice.

~ J.P.

LESSON 2

SEEK RENEWAL IN NATURE

"Those who contemplate the beauty of the earth find reserves of strength that will endure as long as life lasts."

~ Rachel Carson

Although Oprah loves the city of Chicago we've often heard her say that one of her favorite places to be is under a magnificent California oak tree on her Montecito estate, surrounded by her family of dogs. Oprah is truly at home in nature, which has inspired, nurtured and been a source of healing for her.

Oprah invited viewers along on a camping trip to Yosemite to encourage everyone to take time out and enjoy the natural wonders of the world around us. After she watched the astounding documentary series *Planet Earth* she promoted it on her show because she said it made her fall profoundly in love with "her Mother Earth." She later narrated the natural history series *Life* and encouraged us to see Al Gore's documentary on climate change, *An Inconvenient Truth.*

After learning about the horrors of puppy mills, Oprah steered us toward becoming advocates of pet adoption and helped us become better stewards of our dogs by introducing us to some of the best trainers in the business. We cried with Oprah over the loss of her beloved golden retriever, Gracie, even though she said that loss helped her to slow down and appreciate life. Oprah, like many of us, believes that animals help us to become kinder and gentler people.

Oprah has taught us that this Earth is our classroom; that Nature in all its glory allows us breathing space and the means to experience stillness and regeneration. By taking the time to appreciate our natural world, we just might be able to feel the stirrings of our souls and gain new perspective and by learning how to better protect our precious planet we can ensure that Mother Earth will sustain and delight those who come after us.

> *Life whispers to us all the time. Sometimes those whispers happen under the shade of an oak tree or through nuzzles from our angels in fur. The whispers are a hello, a reminder and sometimes a demand for action. Nature gives us so much and asks so little in return.*

Two sudden, startling and far too young deaths in my family just two months apart had left me and my loved ones emotionally frail, deeply bereft and reminded in an unavoidable way about the fleeting nature of the life experience.

A month after the second loss, Nancy visited Spencer and me at our northern Idaho summer retreat. Remembering that Nancy has had a lifelong thing for wolves I planned to take her to visit Wolf People in Cocolalla, less than an hour away from our home. The wolf sanctuary offers visitors an opportunity to spend time with an adult wolf "ambassador" in a penned area adjacent to their shop and information center. For a nominal fee guests can caravan into the hills to meet a dozen more wolves, safely and contentedly living their lives away from gun-toting predators.

When I phoned to reserve a space on the sanctuary tour I was told to come early to play with the babies.

The babies?

Two packs of wolf cubs, one six-weeks-old, the other eight, were on the premises for a few hours each day. What a rare treat this would be for Nancy. She and I both adore dogs and I imagined her joy at getting to meet the ancestors of the animals we love so much.

We arrived nearly an hour before our designated time, not wanting to miss out on the opportunity to say hello to the cubs. I assumed we would be escorted to the pens, a baby wolf placed gently in our arms for a photo op and then we'd be swept off to the hills to meet the main attraction. Instead just the two of us were ushered into a pen with five playful, rambunctious, fanged, silly, soft, tall-eared, awkward and sim-

ply adorable creatures. They nipped at our toes, they played with our clothes, they cuddled with us and we watched in utter amazement as they "wolfed" down their breakfast in a feeding frenzy.

We played with them for nearly an hour. Their mother had rejected them shortly after birth so they seemed to enjoy the attention as much as we did. They were the epitome of life.

This excursion was intended as a gift for my girlfriend yet this dance with nature gave way to something so much more for me. It was a source of renewal in the most unexpected place. I felt a palpable shift away from grief and mourning. I felt life. I had held it in my arms in such a tangible way. The healing had begun.

~ J.P.

LESSON 3

ATTRACT A FORMIDABLE AND FOREVER SIDEKICK

> "The glory of friendship is not the outstretched hand, nor the kindly smile nor the joy of companionship; it is the spiritual inspiration that comes to one when they discover that someone else believes in them and is willing to trust them."
> ~ Ralph Waldo Emerson

Do you have an Ethel for your Lucy? A Sundance for your Butch? A Louise for your Thelma? A sidekick who is there for you through thick and thin? A fiercely loyal companion who loves you for you and not for what you have done for them lately? Oprah has that in Gayle King and never has a friendship been heralded or examined as much as the sparkling intimacy between these two forces of nature.

When Oprah speaks of her best girlfriend she does so with wistfulness, gratitude and admirable affection. Her eyes well and her heart swells. She maintains that Gayle is even happier for her success than she is herself. We believe her because that's the kind of friend we strive to be—supportive and joyous without envy. What an incredibly healthy way to navigate life—to want the very best for your friend. To not display a twinge of jealousy. To be so incredibly openhearted that sharing a friend's joy is just as fulfilling as having your own.

Yes, many of Oprah and Gayle's adventures captured on camera are madcap and filled with torrents of laughter. They spar. They jest. They challenge each other. Yet a friendship this deep and authentic requires a foundation of loyalty, commitment, forgiveness and acceptance far away from audiences and sound bites. It requires nurturing and sensitivity and mindfulness. It requires time and a certain degree of selflessness. All friendships do.

From our front row seat we have watched this friendship weather media skepticism and time and time again we have seen Gayle display steadfast support. We have also seen Oprah return the favor. Thanks to her best friend Gayle has landed a key position at O Magazine, a plucky correspondent gig on the Oprah Show and even her own self-titled OWN program, not to mention the extraordinary perk of having Josh Groban pop in for a surprise visit. Being Oprah's "bestie" is quite a gig.

But after twenty-five years of "Gayle this" and Gayle that" we are left feeling that when it comes to friendship it's Oprah who is truly the lucky one.

> ***Attracting the loyal and loving best friend we want to have in our life begins with being the loyal and loving best friend we know we can be.***

Someone once gave me a pillow embroidered with the words, "You can't make new old friends." It's easy for me to consider new people I've met as the dearest of friends—sometimes I feel so warmed and welcomed in their presence it's as if I've known them forever. My mother used to describe herself as a "people person" and the apple hasn't fallen far from that tree. Still there is something special about an old friend, especially a friend of over sixty years.

I met Michele in pre-school. Our parents knew each other. Phoenix is a big city with a small-town atmosphere and growing up there in the 1950's and 60's was quite an adventure. Michele and I share memories of hatching eggs in kindergarten and taking our baby chicks home, getting teased about our sizes in elementary school, attending Junior Cotillion. In school photos I'm always in the back row with the boys and little gap-toothed Michele is always in the front row. She was called "Twig" long before Twiggy came along.

In high school we were practically inseparable. Whenever Michele ran away from home it was my house she came to. My friends liked to hang out at my house for the well-stocked refrigerator and the delicious Armenian food always in abundance. By the way, no one _ever_ referred to me as "Twig" at any time in my life.

Michele and I and a few other inquisitive sorts did some things no one else was doing in Phoenix at the time. We snuck out of our homes late at night to hear Ray Charles and James Brown perform in haunts on the other side of the tracks. We smoked joints and tried peyote together and lost our virginity at nearly the same time.

College rolled around. I headed to California, Michele went north. She married and had a baby. We checked in maybe only once in a very long time.

Seventeen years passed with zero communication. There were kids, marriages, divorces, careers. Michele had become a college English professor and was attending a party at the home of a colleague, speaking to her colleague's husband when she said, "Byron, you're Armenian aren't you?

He nodded.

"My best friend growing up was Armenian. You wouldn't happen to know the Mehagians in Phoenix would you?"

He did. My mother was married to his uncle.

My mother gave me this news. I called Michele immediately. We were so geographically close for all those years and didn't know it; I was then a single mother and massage therapist in Los Angeles while Michele was a beloved professor right up the coast in Montecito. Copious tears of joy were shed at our reunion.

Now we are there for each other in the most unimaginable of ways. We have taken road trips and enjoyed Paris together. We now celebrate holidays and birthdays together and we can talk about anything at all. We have a shared history—a factor that cannot be manufactured. True friendship is such a blessing and a gift. It provides a mirror of our best selves.

~ N.M.

LESSON 4

READ OFTEN

"Once you learn to read, you will be forever free."
~ Frederick Douglass

There is likely no one in recent history who has done more to encourage reading, for pleasure or enlightenment, than Oprah Winfrey. She has been a godsend to the publishing industry and to our cultural landscape as a whole. Oprah's stamp of approval on a book has created instant best sellers and instant wealth for authors.

From a young age Oprah has sought solace, entertainment and wisdom through books and she has inspired us to follow in her literary footsteps. She has guided us to start our own book clubs, introduced us to little known and first-time authors and revived interest in some of the great classics of literature. Some of her choices pushed us to become better readers.

Oprah has encouraged us to interact and connect with other readers, invited us to dine with some brilliant and challenging authors such as Toni Morrison and has expanded our horizons through her wildly successful web casts with Ekhart Tolle, author of *A New Earth*. We've learned to trust Oprah so much that when she gets behind something we willingly go along with her on the journey. From Oprah has come the idea of reading a book as a shared community.

Will we ever forget meeting George Dawson, grandson of slaves, who first learned to read and write at the age of 98? He mastered his ABC's in two days because he was in such a hurry. He understood the importance of books and wanted to make up for lost time. And because Oprah understands the importance of books, reading and education, will we ever forget learning how many scholarships she has granted over the years, putting her money where her heart is?

> *There is a world of information, inspiration, enlightenment and adventure waiting for us between the covers of books (or on our digital reading devices). Book in hand, you're enriched and entertained. Book in hand, you're never alone.*

My girlfriend Kelly and I often say that we are such voracious readers we will even read every word on a cereal box. I don't ever remember not having a book in motion. I read the Bobbsey Twins series as a little girl, curled up in my bed tearing through the adventures of Nan, Bert, Flossie and Freddie. I couldn't get to the next book fast enough.

I've joined book clubs and have read most of Oprah's offerings. I enjoy long flights. Without computer or phone I dive into a great read as quickly as the plane ascends. Very few lunches or phone calls with friends take place without "What are you reading?" being part of the conversation.

When my husband presented me with an e-reader a few years ago I was aghast. I'm a purist. Doesn't he know that about me? I study the artistry of book covers, I pay attention to paper stock and font choice and read every word on the back cover as well as the spine. An e-book to me seemed like an electronic hug or kiss. The intent is there but without the tactile experience. So it sat.

"Are you ever going to at least give it a try?" he implored. So finally I did. Those of you reading this on your own e-reader already know what I am about to tell you—that my husband in fact really _does_ know me. Now I read even more and with greater ease. When I travel I no longer have to load up my suitcase with heavy books, which becomes especially frustrating with the weight tariffs enforced by airlines. I just load up my Kindle with several titles, toss it in a handbag or backpack and am good to go. Or I'll take my new iPad. I can store thousands of books between the two.

I still buy paperbacks and hard covers. I'll always have a library overflowing with classics and New York Times bestsellers. An undiscovered book remains one of my favorite gifts. And whether I read a cereal box at the breakfast table or State of Wonder on my iPad, I know the ability to read is one of the greatest gifts of being human and that reading is one of the great adventures of our lifetime.

And she lived happily ever after. The end.

~J.P.

LESSON 5

OWN YOURSELF

"You can be anything you want to be, if you only believe with sufficient conviction and act in accordance with your faith; for whatever the mind can conceive and believe, the mind can achieve."

~ Napoleon Hill

A dirt-poor black girl from rural Mississippi. A powerful billionaire with estates in lush Hawaii and lovely Montecito. A voracious reader who loves snuggling at home in comfy clothes and with cuddly pups. A gowned and bejeweled VIP cascading down a red carpet. A woman of influence establishing a school for girls. A coveted commencement speaker in the Ivy League realm. A slender talk show host parading a wagon of fat equivalent to the amount of weight she dropped. A woman struggling with body issues, overcompensating with big hair, big clothes and big accessories. A girl's girl whose best friend knew her before fame and fortune. A woman whose other best friend is American royalty, the former first lady of California. A street reporter who would one day create a media empire. The many sides of Oprah are varied and complex, an improbable exercise in heady contrasts.

Whether we see her as that little girl hungry for knowledge or a media phenomenon who has used her platform to teach, one glimpse into the storybook world of Oprah Winfrey reveals a woman who, simply put, owns herself—her past, her present, her weight, her challenges, her victories, her demons, her influence, her fortune, her future, her empire. She inhabits her show and her life, physically and spiritually.

It was Roger Ebert who opened her eyes to the power of syndication—to literally owning her work. It was Bill Cosby who told her to "sign every check and to know her business." And when you know your business, whether it is your home, your work, your family, your friends or your physical being, you are an empowered participant in your destiny.

Oprah accepts responsibility for that destiny. In owning herself, Oprah stays the course. She doesn't make excuses. She doesn't place blame. When a half-sister entered her life during the final season of the Oprah Winfrey Show, Oprah welcomed this newfound family member onto her set and into her heart with grace and dignity. She didn't shun her sibling. She owned this part of her, stunning and surprising as it was. She took control of what could have been a media blitzkrieg. She made the announcement on her terms, in her own story-telling and empathic way. She, not the tabloids, owned that story. She wouldn't have had it any other way.

> ***Owning oneself is foundational. When we fully accept our past and come to terms with who we are, blemishes and all, we become active shapers of our destiny. We are better armed to face adversity and we have open arms to accept the abundance that comes our way.***

How many Poles does it take? A Pole walked into a bar.

Did you hear one about the Polish family? Yes, I did. Over and over again.

My birth name was Jablonski, emphasis on the "ski.". Growing up in the 1960's Polish jokes were ubiquitous—on the playground, in classrooms, on television and in movies. As children and teens we want nothing more than to fit in. When your last name invites a punch line it does little to endear you to the nuances and significance of your heritage.

What if I run into a crush while walking out of the Polish deli with kielbasa in hand? Would my fourth grade classmates tease me for selecting Poland as my country of choice for an extensive research project? (Actually, some did). Would I ever be able to introduce myself without bracing for some pejorative comment?

It's a delicate balance, owning what we're given and working toward what we want to be. When the lens of sensitivity diminished with age and maturity, fully owning my heritage was a significant milestone. As an additional bonus, I fell in love with and married a man whose parents were both Polish. Together we visited Poland where we explored our ancestors' paths with an enormous sense of pride and wonder. When I heard Polish natives speak, it was as if my grandmother spoke. When I walked into their restaurants, it was a sensory overload—a culinary connection to my childhood. Pierogi never tasted so good.

Owning all aspects of our personal history, guts and glory, is essential to fully realizing the unique experience of who and what we are. I learned that *sitting comfortably atop my Polish roots and all that they represented was a formidable accomplishment marked by pride, curiosity and acceptance.*

The irony? Even though I was deluged with them as a child, I couldn't tell you a single Polish joke today for all the chrusciki in Warsaw.

~ J.P.

LESSON 6

INTENTION

"We choose our joys and sorrows long before we experience them."

~ Kahlil Gibran

At the core of every Oprah show has been a desire to unravel and reveal the intentions behind any given action. She frequently underscored the importance of taking responsibility for one's actions and urged us to remember that living one's life trying to please others results in unwanted consequences.

Oprah didn't always pay attention to intention, as she herself has admitted. When Oprah finally connected those dots and began the segment "Remembering Your Spirit" she uplifted more than our breasts.

There is no greater way to teach than by example and Oprah has learned to align her work with her conscious intention. Only by clearly defining our intentions can we achieve the pure focus we need to achieve our goals, whatever they may be. Achieving goals allows us to become our powerful, authentic selves. What Oprah has achieved she wishes for all of us. She has provided us with roadmaps to success in all areas of our lives. By embracing the idea that our thoughts create our reality, Oprah has led us to dive deeper into our souls.

Tererai Trent, Oprah's favorite guest, is perhaps the most like Oprah. Oprah knew there was a larger life for her beyond rural Mississippi where she grew up and she went on to become one of the most powerful and philanthropic women on the planet. Tererai grew up in a tiny village in Zimbabwe yet dreamed of getting an education, a goal that seemed completely out of reach until a visitor to her village ignited a spark in her. After a forced marriage at age eleven and years of domestic abuse, she came to America, achieved a PhD and is now set to return to her village and start her own school, thanks to a generous grant Oprah made to the project.

What Oprah and Tererai Trent have shown us is that no matter the difficult circumstances of our birth or early lives, if we decide to accomplish great things—if we clearly set our intentions and keep our eyes on the prize—we can prevail. We can change our circumstances and create better lives for ourselves and for others.

> *Intention is a powerful life tool. It's a declaration to ourselves and to the universe that this is what we want, this is why we want it and this is how hard we're willing to work to make it happen. Intention setting requires authenticity, clarity and effort. The payoff? When our dreams manifest we experience profound soul satisfaction.*

It was a sound business model with formidable projections and spreadsheets. My business partner and I set out to launch a chain of community newsweeklies, before the web grabbed the newspaper-reading segment of the marketplace. He would be the publisher, I would be editor. Together we would create a group of hyper-local papers. Between us we had over forty years of newspapering on our resumes and in our blood. It would take mettle and ambition but we were confident we could pull it off.

The spreadsheets were appealing if the economy cooperated and if the local businesses showed support with their ad dollars. Yet the key to the success of this enterprise would not be red or black, awards or notoriety. The mission statement, the intention, was pure—to cultivate a sense of community in a region that felt neglected, to create a platform to honor local heroes (in our book that meant teachers, public servants, students, activists and philanthropists) and to applaud achievement and human spirit.

Each edition reflected that goal. Amid the intricacies of covering local politics, the flash of Hollywood's proximity that saw famous faces in our pages weekly and the standard news and reviews, each and every issue heralded something or someone special—an octogenarian marathon runner, twin brothers determined to carve a path of altruism, artists, writers, athletes and epicureans—all contributing to their community selflessly and passionately.

Nothing signaled our commitment to that vision more than a letter we received from a parent of a six-year-old. His child's classmate had been killed by *a wayward driver while walking home from school. The incident continued to haunt the children who witnessed the death and lost a friend and schoolmate. The local broadcast news gave the horror thirty seconds of airtime and the daily newspaper ran a short news item. None of the coverage was satisfying. Could we help honor her life in some way?*

Through my shock and sadness I telephoned him and told him "Yes, absolutely" we would honor his request. I asked him to give me a few days to gather thoughts. The responsibility was large and looming. Yes, we could write an expanded story on her short life filled with as many pictures as her family could bear, but that didn't feel right. Obituaries shouldn't exist for six-year-old girls.

After some quiet contemplation it became clear what needed to be done. Valentine's Day was on the horizon. Children typically bring cards to school, handmade or store bought, one for each student in their class. Her absence would be pronounced as they sat down to address their missives. I asked the parent to facilitate a Valentine's Day project—to have the children each write a Valentine sentiment to their gone-but-not-forgotten friend. On a sole page of the newspaper we printed a beautiful photo of the girl and all of the sweet messages from her classmates.

I wept the day that paper was printed because we had the ability to honor her life and we did so in a way that was pure and meaningful. Intention was served. It was our most honorable moment.

~ J.P.

LESSON 7

LOVE IS IN THE DETAILS

"Let the beauty we love be what we do. There are hundreds of ways to kneel and kiss the ground."
~ Rumi

The packages gleamed. Not a blinding gleam but rather an appealing presence that elicited a gasp, a wow, a caffeine jolt of joy. It's Oprah's Favorite Things episode and the stage is overflowing with spectacularly wrapped gift packages. It was during her final year on the air that Oprah let us in on a little secret: these lovely parcels were not wrapped in holiday paper. Instead, her staff meticulously wrapped the gifts in fabric. This way, she confided, the studio lights wouldn't end up bouncing off highly reflective paper creating an unsightly glare.

Oprah's desire to deliver a pretty panoramic stems from her affection for her audience and viewers. And love, in its purest form, is in the details.

It was in the comfortable green room, the cozy "on-deck" haven she and her staff created for guests of the show. Whether Oprah made an appearance in the green room before airtime or not her imprint was all over it. Her guests were welcomed with a big green hug that said, "We're glad you're here."

It was in her opening segment, her studio, her road trips, her surprises (but wait, there's more!) It was in the tenderness of her preparation ("I read your book last night" or "I saw your movie.")

It was in the handshake, the hug, the kiss that welcomed guests to her stage and to her world, inviting them to fully participate in the community she's created.

And it was in all the glory of her final season. She reunited the casts of *The Color Purple, The Sound of Music, Love Story* and *The Way We Were* and our hearts sang. She took a grateful audience to Australia. She repeatedly honored staff, former guests and viewers with detailed dignity, folly and love. She admittedly even neglected the launch of her OWN network to give the final season her focus and heart. And that she did. A sonnet for the senses, it was, wrapped with rich satisfaction. What a lovely parting gift to us all.

> *When we are mindful and keenly aware of the magnitude of even the smallest gestures we are expressing love with tender and meaningful care. Large gestures can be shallow and empty if we neglect the nuance of the small details that say, "I took the time because I care."*

Every year the advertising sales department of the LA Weekly newspaper would host a rousing holiday dinner at a fancy restaurant. They were a motley crew, my team of creative, cunning and dynamic sales people. Long hours, demanding clients and unforgiving deadlines made for an often stressful workload, but together we got the work done and the annual holiday dinner was a way to honor the team and release some steam.

As Associate Publisher I was aware that some of the staff got along and some did not. Many were supportive of the efforts of their peers but others were envious of their colleagues' success. One year when the staff was assailed with special project after special project and work piled on top of more work, I decided to express my gratitude with a special gift – one that required thought and detail.

Six weeks before the dinner I distributed a sheet of paper to each employee at a Monday morning meeting. On that sheet appeared the name of every member of the advertising staff and nothing more. Their assignment? Write down three positive things about each person on the list. That was all I said.

"I know what you're doing," one piped up. "You want to prove that it's possible to find three nice things to say about anyone."

"It's an experiment, right?" asked another. "You want to see how creative and descriptive we can be, like when we're creating an ad for a client."

No and no. With no further questions everyone submitted the assignment before the designated deadline, curiosity clearly getting the best of them.

It's the night of the holiday dinner. One by one the staff, dressed to the nines, walks into the swanky private room of a seaside bistro. Typically it's a free-for-all and people sit wherever they want. This year there were oversized place cards, with a photo of each employee designating their assigned seat. As people found their photos some started squealing. Some were silent. Some were laughing. Some got a little weepy. It took a few moments for the collective "light bulb" to go off. When it did, there was a moment of astounding revelation. The frames for their photos were made up of all of the things their fellow employees had said about them: "empathetic listener," "hysterically funny," "an amazing mother," "a terrific salesperson," "nice hair." "beautiful eyes," "the biggest heart I know." Each had about twenty descriptions, a bounty of compliments from their peers. There was a palpable shift and it carried over into the workplace long after the dinner.

A dozen years later some tell me that place card is still among their most prized possessions.

~ J.P.

LESSON 8

WHEN YOU KNOW BETTER, YOU DO BETTER

"If you can't make a mistake you can't make anything."
~Marva Collins

Oprah claims this is one of the most important lessons she herself learned in twenty-five years.

We agree with the sentiment yet a touch of irony comes into play. By watching how Oprah treated one particular guest we learned that sometimes, just because you have a platform and power doesn't mean you have to wield them.

James Frey duped Oprah and legions of readers before news broke that elements of his memoir, *A Million Little Pieces,* were largely fabricated. Oprah had named his tome one of her coveted book club selections, further boosting already lofty sales and helping to establish his credibility as an author. Yet months later it was revealed that when Frey appeared on Oprah's show he had lied to her about the authenticity of the book's content. Oops. When rumblings about a possible hoax first surfaced Oprah further defended him on a *Larry King Live* appearance. Oops again. It was a headline-making and embarrassing moment for Oprah.

Oprah brought Frey to her show for a second appearance that ultimately became a public flogging. He said he thought the topic would be redemption and later claimed he felt ambushed. It turned out to be her most controversial show ever. Spiritual teacher and friend Marianne Williamson even called Oprah out on her actions, asking her "Who do you think you are?"

When Oprah brought Frey back for a two-part installment among her final ten shows, it seemed she did so to honor her innate compassion—the compassion that was lacking five years earlier when she used her platform to chastise him. In the end, the greatest moment in the whole debacle came when Oprah was moved to tears by her own admission that she failed to bring compassion to that second interview. Her evolved self was disappointed in the behavior of her earlier self. When she asked for the cameras to be cut because her composure was waning, it was Frey who reached out to comfort her with a hug. In the end, it was about redemption—for Oprah and for James Frey.

> *As ever-evolving beings our strength lies in our ability to learn from past mistakes. It's never too late to analyze our behavior and rectify old or continuing wrongs. In the words of Oprah's wise friend Maya Angelou, "When you know better, you do better."*

I've never called myself a healer though others have. After more than thirty-five years working as a massage therapist, Jin Shin Jyutsu practitioner and teacher I think of myself as someone who assists in the healing process and that the only true healing is self-healing. Still, I have often been drawn to people in need, especially in my personal relationships. One day I hit a brick wall.

The man I lived with and was madly in love with had a drinking problem. He hadn't touched alcohol for the first several weeks we'd known each other. Then one day he came home with a bottle of Southern Comfort. I'd never seen him take a drink and, except for the occasional glass of wine with dinner, I was basically a teetotaler. He emptied that bottle in no time at all.

Under the influence my sweet lover became a force of nature—wild, uncontrollable, overpowering. His transformation was dramatic, like Popeye after a can of spinach or the Hulk when he got mad. Once Pandora's box had been opened, the drinking continued until I was in such despair that I finally went to my first meeting of Al-Anon, an organization founded to help friends and relatives of alcoholics.

Someone read a list of Al-Anon Dos and Don'ts. Turns out I was doing every single one of the don'ts. At first I didn't tell my boyfriend where I was going when I went to meetings. Then my behavior began to change. I stopped nagging. I pretended to ignore the alcohol. I did what was suggested—I took my eyes off of my alcoholic and focused them on myself.

The first and perhaps most important lesson I learned in Al-Anon was how to say "no" without feeling *guilty. I'd heard the phrase "people pleaser" bandied about and I definitely fit that description. I wanted to be liked. I wanted to help people, often at my own expense. Mary, my Jin Shin Jyutsu teacher, had once said, "You can't give unless you have." I had been giving to the point of exhaustion.*

Once I knew better, I stopped enabling my alcoholic. A few months after I entered Al-Anon, my boyfriend entered rehab and became an active member of AA.

~ N.M.

LESSON 9

TAKE RISKS

"Man cannot discover new oceans unless he has the courage to lose sight of the shore."
~ Andre Gide

Oprah exudes courage and bravery, never shying away from controversial topics or embarrassing personal stories and she has guided her viewers along the same path of unflinching honesty. By sharing her shortcomings and the methods she has employed to overcome them, she has helped us become more open and inspired us to take chances and live our best lives.

As Oprah listens to others reveal their hidden secrets without judgment, we have become less judgmental in the process. When we are no longer afraid to become the people we were meant to be, we are ready to challenge ourselves to take those leaps of faith and to risk changing those things about ourselves that we are able to change.

So many of us have ventured out of our comfort zones and embraced new careers, healthier diets, new hairstyles and clothing or new home décor because of someone or something we saw on Oprah. Her "A-Team" of advisors, experts and gurus has guided us on a journey of renewal by helping us see things differently.

When Oprah made the leap into daytime television in Chicago, she overcame her doubt and fear through the fundamental belief that we can achieve our dreams. Twenty-five years later we know how that turned out. The only constant in life is change and change relies on taking risks. There has been no end of inspirational every day people whose stories have been told on air to provide us with the motivation we need to transform ourselves as well as the world around us.

On one particularly moving show Oprah reunited the remaining Freedom Riders and we were able to witness and pay tribute to the bravest of souls who risked life and limb to fight for the civil rights of all men and woman. The courageous actions they chose to undertake transformed the civil rights movement and provided tears of gratitude and inspiration for all who witnessed their journey.

No one can force another person to change yet Oprah knows that we can plant the seeds of change and introduce people to looking at things in a new way. As she has often said, she's just the messenger. People must ultimately make decisions for themselves.

> *Risk-taking becomes easier if we hold fast to our dreams, change our fears into fun and turn our problems into projects. Nothing great has ever been accomplished without taking risks.*

I came of age during the turbulence of the 1960's—Vietnam, political assassinations, violent protests, sex, drugs and rock and roll. After a trip to Europe to study Italian, I returned stateside and reentered college but I couldn't settle down. I had seen enough of the world to know I wanted to see more and as a love and peace espousing hippie I wanted to be somewhere far away from the all the turmoil going on around me.

I followed the siren's call and landed on Ibiza, a beautiful Spanish island in the Mediterranean. The year was 1969 and I was twenty-one years old.

Ibiza felt like home to me. I picked up the Spanish language with facility and met other like-minded souls from all parts of the globe. The little money that I had would not last long and I wanted to find a way to stay on this island paradise. My primary talent at the time was being able to cook, a skill inherited from my mother, who learned in the kitchen of her mother. That skill has served me well over the years. Everybody has to eat.

I decided that what my little island home needed most was a healthy vegetarian restaurant. Within no time I became the owner of an apartment that was to be converted into one, thanks to the generosity of a young man I had been cooking for. Five months later, my restaurant opened.

I knew nothing about running a restaurant and little more about vegetarian cooking besides how to make brown rice and vegetables. It was a trial by fire, literally. Yet for the next three years, with a little help from my friends, we served some wonderful meals to crowds of amazing people,

They say ignorance is bliss. If I'd known how much hard work goes into running a restaurant would I have taken on the task? Perhaps not. Instead I leapt into the unknown, discovered I had a passion for feeding people and had the time of my life.

~ N. M.

LESSON 10

GIVE FREELY, RECEIVE GRACIOUSLY

"I have found that among its other benefits, giving liberates the soul of the giver."
~ Maya Angelou

Oh... the much-anticipated Favorite Things episode. We watched with a pearl of envy each December as Oprah's jolly helpers paraded through Harpo Studio's aisles with humongous sackfuls of gifts hand-picked by Oprah—things she loved, things she ate, things she wore and things she was itching to share. It was a veritable three-ring circus with Oprah serving as ringmaster. And it was hard to miss the Cheshire Cat smile of satisfaction that spread across her face as she watched her audience react with a wild fervor that fell somewhere in between loopy and catatonic.

Yes, Oprah had the power and the pull to secure big-ticket items from manufacturers. The tally for the loot didn't exactly show up on her personal American Express platinum account but that spirit of generosity was at the core of the show's heart. Life-changing information, life-changing inspiration and life-altering gifts were doled out. The deep pockets of her platform allowed her to give in a very large way, and she did, again and again. Cars! Trips!

Homes! Education! Honeymoons! Her generosity knew no limits and if the giving was a surprise, all the better.

For years we witnessed Oprah's joy in giving and for those paying close attention the lesson was clear: giving is receiving. Talk about an "aha" moment. Oprah's joy in giving was in direct proportion to the joy she received in doing so. The bigger the bang for the recipient, the bigger the bang for Oprah. When tears flowed, Oprah got misty. When guests or audience members jumped, Oprah got a little bouncy. When they screamed, she ignited.

We also learned from Oprah the profound impact made by giving of oneself; a smile, a compliment, a look in the eye of complete recognition that says to another, "You exist. You matter." Receiving and, doing so graciously, is simply the other side of the giving coin.

Guests often waxed poetic about Oprah's influence, power, fortune and fame. For years she responded with a dismissal, a "pshaw" or a quick change of subject. But over time, as she evolved, as she settled into the Oprahness of being Oprah, she received these sentiments differently. A compliment was met with a "thank you" or an "I honor that."

> *How can we give, how can we surprise, how can we change lives with an extension of self? And when offered a gift or a compliment, instead of instinctively batting it away, we need to honor the gracious intent behind it and keep two key words close to vest: the "thank you" in receiving brings the giving full circle.*

When I was fifteen years old I received a small allowance, had a few babysitting jobs and was a junior apprentice to our local Avon lady. I spent my earnings on clothing, records, lip gloss and my baby sister. Six years my junior, I showered Jennifer with little gifts—a Little Kiddles doll tucked inside a plastic ice cream cone, a shiny ring, a delectable confection. To a little girl it was a treasure trove.

To my Depression Era grandmother, however, it was wasteful. Gram opined on just about everything under the sun but typically offered little criticism of her grandchildren. So I was pretty surprised when she cornered me one day with an offer. Come to think of it, perhaps it was more of a dare. She would match every penny I could save in the course of one year. "You're too generous" she told me. She wanted to teach me a lesson.

I had every intention of making good on our deal. I thought I could reel in the generosity. The savings lasted for about a month. I bought gifts for family and friends. I donated money to March of Dimes and Muscular Dystrophy Association. When I gave my Gram a birthday card she looked at the price on the back and muttered a "tsk, tsk." She never once asked me how our little deal was coming along but when we visited her over the summer and I splurged on a ton of stuff for Jennifer at the local five and dime, I suspect she knew it wasn't going so well. I didn't learn the lesson she sought to teach me. Giving brought me far more pleasure than amassing any great wealth. I looked at abundance as a game of hot potato. The minute it hit my hand, I wanted to pass it on to someone else. Giving *felt good. At the end of the year I presented her with my meager savings passport and she gave me the equally meager matching amount. We never spoke of it again.*

Twenty years later I was working as an assistant to the associate publisher for the LA Weekly. A single mom worked alongside me in the advertising department. She was often late to work because she did not own a car and between getting her young son to school and navigating public transit it was a two-hour journey at best. One morning she was a puddle of tears when our boss told her she would lose her job if she were late one more time. I took her into the parking lot and walked over to my car. "Here," I said handing her the keys. "It's yours." I was planning on getting a new car that weekend, trading in my first ever car for a gently used coupe. I never told my grandmother about giving my car away but apparently my mother did. When I next visited Gram at the retirement village she gave me a hug and said. "You did a good thing," then changed the subject.

When I was honored for my giving and charity work years later, it was a curious experience. I had to learn to receive the honor graciously. It was a big to do at the Motion Picture Arts and Sciences building. I was surrounded by family and friends. Thoughts of "am I worthy of this?" filled my head. When my grandmother wrote to tell me how proud she was of me being honored for giving, the dots were connected. With all of the giving that I have done in my lifetime, it was a complete circle only because the recipients all received graciously. So I did just that.

~J.P.

LESSON 11

AGE GRATEFULLY

"People are like stained-glass windows. They sparkle and shine when the sun is out, but when the darkness sets in, their true beauty is revealed only if there is a light from within."
~ Elizabeth Kubler-Ross

Never one to hide her age, Oprah has instead reveled in the spiritual growth and wisdom that comes with aging gracefully and has made a point of fully enjoying the benefits that have accrued with each decade of her life. She has maintained her dignity and has not succumbed to the ever-present push toward plastic surgery so prevalent in our society, although she doesn't condemn those who do. Oprah has chosen instead to follow the examples set by her own mentors like Maya Angelou (who famously commented, "Eighty-two is hot. Eighty-two is fabulous.") and Sidney Poitier. Oprah knows she stands on the shoulders of those who came before her and has always acknowledged her debt to them. As much as she loves to teach, she perhaps loves to learn even more.

When Oprah brought together Teri Hatcher, Cybill Shepherd and Linda Evans, all celebrated beauties who have grown older with grace and dignity, she invited us to take notes on some rare candid talk about the realities of aging. Despite the airbrushed portraits that grace magazine covers, these actresses said there should be no shame in the fact that women don't remain youthful and flawless forever.

Oprah herself dropped the veil of pretense when she allowed us to see her in the early morning, in her flannel pajamas and without makeup. And just to show viewers that it takes a village to get her camera-ready, Oprah let us in on that process too. She let us see for ourselves that peoples' exteriors are not necessarily what they seem and that what matters is what's inside our hearts. That we can show people who we really are. That life is short and so it's all the more important that we live authentically and not fight the aging process and that it is possible to change the way we look at ourselves and learn to love the image we see in our mirrors.

> ***With attention paid to our inner lives, our health and our spirits we can project a beauty that is beyond age. Our inner beauty is the true gold and external adornment is but an expression of our confidence and creativity.***

I turned fifty last year. Half a century. It didn't seem so long ago that my sisters planned a surprise fiftieth birthday celebration for our mother. How could it be my turn already?

I invited fifty of my closest girlfriends to a tea at the beautiful Langham Huntington in Pasadena. I didn't want a flashy affair, just to be surrounded by the beauty of gardens and my beloved posse of female friends. I pictured an afternoon of easy elegance, love and laughter, really good food and unusual tea. I pictured standing in the cozy salon and telling these amazing women what they meant to me and I did just that. What a gift to be able to collectively tell my friends how much I love them. It was deeply satisfying.

Moments afterward Kelly, who had been maid of honor at my wedding and Pam, a dear friend visiting from Puerto Rico, stood up and said, "Now it's our turn." For the next hour or so my girlfriends each poured out their hearts, telling me in their own dramatic, emotional, crazy and loving ways exactly what I meant to them. There was a lot of laughter and there were many tears. I was overwhelmed by the sweetness of the gesture. I felt the love on a cellular level. My cheeks hurt from smiling, my belly ached from laughing and my heart had a Grinch thing going on – it expanded out of chest, just to hold all that love sent my way.

This, it seems, is what aging gratefully is about. Not yammering on about the wrinkles, the gray hair, the physical and psychological shifts. It's about knowing what true abundance is and honoring it wholly and fully. It's feeling confident in your choices and settling comfortably into them all. And it's looking into the future, not into a mirror, and saying, "Bring it on! I've done the work. I'm still a work in progress and I'm ready for whatever awaits."

~ J.P.

LESSON 12

EMBRACE A SPIRITUAL QUEST

"This is my simple religion. There is no need for temples; no need for complicated philosophy. Our own brain, our own heart is our temple; the philosophy is kindness."

~ Dalai Lama

Like a master gardener, Oprah has taught us to cultivate our higher natures, encouraged us to follow a more fulfilling path and develop those qualities of empathy, compassion and tolerance. Only when we develop compassion and tolerance for those who differ from us will we be able us to serve our true purpose as spiritual beings having a human experience.

When Oprah introduced us to trailblazers like Pema Chodron, Thich Nhat Hanh and Gary Zukav, she became a trailblazer herself. We have watched her spiritual beliefs evolve over time. Luckily for us, Oprah has used her platform to introduce us to those who have influenced her most profoundly during her life. Her eagerness to broaden our spiritual horizons has helped us grow immeasurably. We have learned that what matters most is what's inside us and that inner wisdom is more precious than wealth. Will we ever forget the "heart songs" of young poet Mattie Stepanek, who proved that spiritual teachers come in all sizes, ages and faiths?

Embarking on a spiritual quest requires us to first put our own houses in order and then use our lives to help others which is a natural consequence of being our authentic selves. Oprah has urged us to think about creating a physical space for ourselves that is just ours, where we can go on a daily basis to keep a gratitude journal, meditate or pray or read books that inspire us. That this soul work is what is required of us as human beings. If Oprah can carve out that time and space to achieve balance and equilibrium in her busy life, so can we.

> *Engaging in a relationship with what we cannot necessarily see but we know deep within is the foundation of spiritual awakening. Just like a relationship with another person or animal, the relationship with our spiritual self must be nurtured and ever evolving. It cannot be neglected, not even for a day. It requires time, focus and practice. For many it's the part of self that's neglected most and yet it's often the missing link to feeling whole and complete. It expands our thinking and our way of living. It makes us feel part of something quite spectacular. It makes us feel anything is possible.*

I admit it. I was a bit of the wild child who gave my wonderful, loving and conservative parents absolute fits. I was brought up in a Baptist church; later we became Methodists. When asked, at age twelve, if I wanted to join the church I said, "No," and that was it. Though I didn't realize it at the time I was a seeker interested in actual spiritual experience and not just blind belief.

In my late teens I became a vegetarian, more for spiritual reasons than for health, and thus my spiritual quest began. Initially I looked to others for answers—psychics, astrologers and all manner of spiritual teachers. I tried Transcendental Meditation and read every spiritual book I could get my hands on. As I read and studied and matured and especially when I learned to meditate and trust my own instincts I discovered the answers I sought were always within. Others could only confirm those truths, the confirmation usually occurring with what a friend of mine calls "the goose bump factor."

It wasn't until I traveled to Nepal in 1970 and first encountered Tibetan Buddhists that I truly found a religion that resonated with me. The Tibetan refugees I met there were so pure and gentle, resolved to maintain their faith and culture in spite of the persecution that had been inflicted upon them.

Over the years I have been blessed to receive teachings from the Dalai Lama on several occasions. Once, in Los Angeles, at the end of a teaching session, the Dalai Lama was answering random questions from the audience. Someone asked, "What is the fastest way to get enlightened?" There was laughter from the audience and I was thinking to myself that only in Los Angeles would anyone ask such a question. The Dalai Lama, seated cross-legged on his chair, held his face in his hands and bent forward. It seemed that he was laughing himself but when he rose up again I was sitting close enough to see that he was crying. He proceeded to tell us the story of Tibet's great Yogi and saint, Milarepa.

Milarepa had committed terrible deeds in his youth. Fortune led him to Marpa, a great teacher and hard taskmaster. Before he died, Marpa's final teaching to his student was to bend over and show him the calluses on his ass, formed through years of sitting meditation.

My own spiritual quest remains a lifelong journey though over time my beliefs have become far simpler. I know I will never have calluses on my behind since I actually prefer walking meditation. I do know for sure that spiritual growth is the true work of our lives.

~ N.M.

LESSON 13

UNDERSTAND KARMIC LAW

"Karma isn't fate. Nor is it a punishment imposed on us by some external agent. We create our own karma. Karma is the result of the choices we make every moment of every day."
~ Tulku Thondup

As children we learned the Golden Rule: *Do unto others as you would have them do unto you.* If anyone has learned to live by this rule it is Oprah Winfrey. Her staff works like the devil for her because they are co-creators of the same dream—the dream of a better world, the dream of helping people improve their situations and their lives, the dream of living joyously and as part of a single global family. That is the reason, plain and simple, why the Oprah Winfrey Show has held sway for so long. The entire team, inspired by Oprah herself, created a product from which they, in turn, can learn and benefit.

And here it comes again, the idea of intention. As we intend and then act, we create our own karma. *Karma* is a Sanskrit word that means "action," and indeed it is the same principle embodied in Isaac Newton's Third Law of Motion (to every action there is always an equal and opposite reaction.) The Law of Karma can be found in all religions. Truth is truth. Nothing could be simpler than this law of cause and effect. What we put out into the world comes back to us in manifold ways. In essence we are all creators of our own life gardens so we must take care to plant the right seeds. If we are leading with love, generosity and kindness, we are creating conditions that lead to health, peace and prosperity. If we are mired in negative emotions like anger, fear, greed and hate, we are creating the conditions for strife, misery and suffering. As Oprah has said many times, "If you do right, right will follow." Karma is the simple law that governs our universe.

> ***Ultimately, we are each responsible for the quality of our lives. When we fully accept that responsibility we come to understand that our actions, thoughts and deeds can help or hinder our personal relationships and growth as spiritual beings.***

My mother was ninety when she came to live with me. Her memory was fading and she could no longer drive or live on her own. My brother and sister-in-law lived in another state and after lengthy discussions with them about the few options available to us regarding Mom's living situation and care, I finally threw in the towel and gave Mom what she really wanted. She would live with her family. My grown daughter moved back home to help.

My mother and I had never really seen eye-to-eye though I loved her deeply and had always admired her strength and spunk. She was, however, a self-proclaimed "worry wart." As for me, my attitude is more like Bobby McFerrin's; "Don't worry, be happy."

As someone who has always valued my freedom (I've been single and self-employed for most of my life) it wasn't easy having Mom here, even with help from my daughter. I bit my tongue a lot. I counted to ten. At times I snapped. No one could get under my skin (or in my heart) like my mother. I did my best, though my patience was tested and admittedly was lacking at times.

For those who know better, karma can be rather instant as it was in my case. One day as I hiked with my dogs in the hills where I'd been hiking for over twenty years, I had an overwhelming feeling of being trapped. I was thinking of a friend I'd recently visited whose parents had died. She had flexibility and freedom. She had a tension-free home. And she was able to travel the globe and have a life. I felt stuck and I was jealous. And then it happened. I slid on loose gravel and fell into a rut, twisting my ankle. I cursed. I screamed. Using a self-help technique I even grabbed my opposite wrist to relieve the excruciating pain.

Hikers came running to help me up. Two men carried me down the rest of the hill while I apologized to them for not hitting the gym more often. A woman who was clearly afraid of dogs led my dogs Buddha and Cisco down the hill. One of the men got my car, backed it up to the path and put my dogs inside. I insisted I was fine to drive the two or three miles home. Flexing my right ankle to press the gas pedal had me moaning in pain by the time I pulled into my driveway. My daughter called the paramedics and they took me to the emergency room. An X-ray showed I had broken my fibula. I swear it was more painful than childbirth. Loaded up with pain killers and a heavy walking boot on my leg I came home and had the next three months of healing, bed rest and dependency to think about how my negative attitude had brought about my current condition. It was as if the universe had said, "You feel trapped? Try this!" The words to one of John Lennon's songs rang through my head:

*"Instant Karma's gonna get you,
Gonna knock you right on the head,
You better get yourself together,
Pretty soon you're gonna be dead."*

~N.M.

LESSON 14

CREATE JOY AND LAUGH OFTEN

"Sometimes your joy is the source of your smile, but sometimes your smile can be the source of your joy."
~ Thich Nhat Hanh

Oprah is one very funny woman and she knows it. She even said so once on her show, to Sarah Ferguson, the Duchess of York. "I'm funny." She said it as if we, her viewers, didn't already know that. For decades Oprah has laughed at famous funny people from Chris Rock to Jim Carrey to Ellen DeGeneres. She has laughed with her famous friends Julia Roberts, Tom Hanks and John Travolta and she has laughed at herself with the kind of laugh that was infectious, even if you missed the punch line. On a Yosemite camping trip with Gayle we watched her squeeze limes with her mouth for her beloved Moscow Mules. That was nothing compared to the happy dance she did around the iPad that descended from the ceiling, festooned with angel wings, in preparation for her final Favorite Things episode. Oprah can be goofy, silly and downright hilarious.

There is no doubt that Oprah has achieved a black belt in having fun. She loves bringing joy to other peoples' lives whether on her show or in her private life. For Maya Angelou's 70th birthday she organized a weeklong Caribbean cruise. In 2005 she held a three-day celebration honoring twenty-five African-American women who achieved excellence in the arts, entertainment and civil rights causes, and, because she always wanted to have a party with hats, she threw a garden party to remember—fantasy hats and all. And it goes without saying that Oprah's Favorite Things shows are legendary in and of themselves. With all of these gestures Oprah reminds us over and over again that it's okay to celebrate life and cultivate joy, even in the midst of difficulties, hardships or chaos. As Oprah herself once said, "The more you praise and celebrate your life, the more there is in life to celebrate."

> *Gut-busting tears of laughter are one of life's greatest joys. Surround yourself with those who make you laugh. Participate in activities just for the fun of it. Create joy, attract joy and live in your joy and you'll be happier, more fulfilled and healthier. Laughter is free but its benefits are priceless.*

My friend Glenna and I are opposites in so many ways, like Mutt and Jeff. She's African, from Sierra Leone, so she's Black. I'm Armenian. My ancestors come from the Caucasus Mountains. Need I say more? Glenna, however, believes I'm Black too since I always travel with a stash of Tabasco sauce.

Glenna is so tiny that even when size 0's started to show up in stores they still looked too big for her. Her thong underwear looks like lacy dental floss while I'm built for comfort so my booty requires a lot more material. Glenna lives in London but hates the cold. I live in Los Angeles and can't take the heat. The things that Glenna can't eat are most of the things I cook with—tomatoes, lemons, soy sauce, salt. We're a right old pair.

With all our differences what Glenna and I share the most is our sense of optimism and fun. No matter what is going on around us we will both look for the bright side of things. We have been through a lot together over the past thirty years but mostly we laugh. We laugh until we wet ourselves—a thigh slapping, stomach-clutching, snorting, howling-until-we-cry kind of laughter. During one of Glenna's visits my mother had a fall and broke her hip, necessitating a stay in a skilled nursing facility. Whenever we went to visit her we always did our best to bring some smiles and laughter to Mom as well as the other residents.

I can't imagine my life without my friends and family, my adorable dogs, doing work that helps people to feel better, listening to great music and eating delicious food that has been lovingly prepared. Shared pleasure is the true joy of life. I've learned that laughter is good *for the liver and cleanses our souls. That a simple upturn of the mouth, a smile, positively affects all the functions of the body. Spreading joy is one of the most rewarding activities I can think of.*

~ N.M.

LESSON 15

I NEVER THOUGHT OF IT THAT WAY BEFORE

"Change your thoughts and you change your world."
~ Norman Vincent Peale

She was inconsolable. Her body language was deflated and defeated. Her face spoke of crushing fatigue and aching sadness. Jo Ann Compton was tormented by the loss of her daughter, murdered ten years earlier and was so deep in her unrelenting grief that she was incapable of inhaling even the tiniest breath of life. She was neglecting her other daughter, very much alive and needy. She couldn't feel her way toward the path of establishing a new normal, of finding the footing to somehow move on. She had even contemplated taking her own life. That is, until she appeared on The Oprah Winfrey Show and Dr. Phil offered her a life-altering perspective. Instead of mourning her daughter's death why not honor her life? Through her unforgiving pain, through her sorrow and confusion, Jo Ann uttered seven words that would be a sea change for Oprah and her viewers: "I never thought of it that way."

This ideology became the cornerstone of Oprah's vision—not only to educate, but also to impart a shift in thinking. Because when we transcend our habitual patterns of thought we open the doors for evolution to occur. That is when we allow fear and paralysis to exit the psyche to be replaced with hope and action.

We are so often mired in our dogma, in our history, in the way we've always done it or the way we've always thought. Oprah taught us that the greatest "aha" moments are revealed when we dare to think or act differently than we have in the past. The result? A sense of enlightenment that brings peace and understanding. An awareness that calms, enriches and infuses our lives with a welcome beam of light.

> *Even an unthinkable loss is survivable when we focus on life and not loss. When we dare to consider an alternative way of thinking or living, we allow ourselves to navigate the world with possibility and optimism. When we think differently, we live differently.*

Nancy and I were relaxing on the dock of my home in Idaho reveling in the beauty of the trees, the geese and ducks and the meandering river. We were keeping a watchful eye out for a bald eagle, working on this book and musing about life. I mentioned an email I had received earlier that morning from an acquaintance, requesting an hour or two of my time to assist in a project with a looming deadline. A mutual friend had told him I'd be a good resource and I'm usually willing to help when time permits.

Truthfully I wasn't exactly eager to spend two hours on the phone talking about something that really didn't interest me when I was in my Idaho bliss. But I was going to do it because I'm accustomed to helping when asked.

"You know," Nancy said to me, "people will take as much as you're willing to give. You get to decide how much that is."

Talk about a lightning bolt. Really? Boing. Zap. Kaching. Bull's eye. I had never, ever thought of it that way before.

What was I willing to give? An email that would take fifteen or twenty minutes to compose, outlining suggestions to help move his project forward. And that's exactly what I did. "I hope this helps" was how I closed the email. Thirty minutes later I received a grateful reply thanking me for all of the guidance I'd provided. Apparently he met his deadline and my information helped him negotiate a terrific deal.

Some might call this setting boundaries. How far can you stretch yourself without resentment or compromise? For me it's a graceful understanding. I am generous. I enjoy sharing brain cells. I enjoy being of service. Yet I never before considered my role in the perpetuation of some of the give and take of my life. This subtle shift in thinking allows me to be more in concert with my time and my generosity. I am reminded that I always have a choice.

~ J.P.

LESSON 16

DON'T LET MOMENTS DEFINE YOU, LET THEM DIVINE YOU

> "Life shrinks or expands in proportion to one's courage."
>
> ~ Anais Nin

She lost her three children in a horrific car accident. He was a college junior, caught in the line of fire during a campus massacre. They escaped the genocide in Rwanda as young girls, hiding in trees and fearing for their lives and the safety of their friends and families. Unthinkable fate. Unfathomable pain. Unspeakable terror. And all guests on *The Oprah Winfrey Show*.

Oprah shied away from the salacious but not from the human condition. With compassion and strength she helped emotionally frail guests put their pain into words. With assistance from Dr. Phil and other experts who became part of her insightful posse, Oprah helped them see hope through their anguish. In doing so she shed light on the perseverance of the human spirit. She helped us all to see that tragedy does not have to define us. It can "divine" us. Oprah has exposed us to the power of living beyond tragedy and rising above pain. We saw that surviving tragedy makes people stronger. That it gives a renewed sense of purpose. It may even offer appreciation and gratitude that was absent before. Above all she showed us there's no shame in seeking joy in simple moments when grief is seemingly impossible to bear.

Oprah showed us that it takes faith and purpose and community to move on. It takes action to heal. And it takes a gentle bath of self-love to brave the waters of fate—to live out loud once again and to live the new normal thrust upon us.

The family who lost their three children miraculously gave birth to triplets. The college student vowed to make it harder for "dangerous people to buy guns." The young Rwandan girls found their way to America and were reunited with their surviving family members on Oprah's show in a moment of ecstasy and hopefulness.

> *It takes courage and time to move beyond paralyzing loss and pain. Oprah has reminded us that we are only truly healed when we translate suffering into action, for that's when we transcend the role of victim and blaze a trail of survivorship and strength.*

Three years earlier she lost both her breasts to cancer. She was on her way to a funeral for her college roommate, a thirty-year-old woman who had lost her own battle with cancer a week before.

"Why me?" cried the petite blonde sitting next to me on that flight from Los Angeles to Chicago. I listened with compassion and comfort as my grief-stricken seatmate poured out buckets of emotion and tears.

After a moment or two of silence, I asked her: "Why you?"

She looked at me curiously—eyes squinted, face scrunched, head cocked. "Why me?" she repeated.

"Yes," I said. "Why you? You beat the odds. Your friend didn't. You're a survivor not a victim." I told her that if she saw herself as a survivor she could harness an unparalleled strength. She could live in gratitude instead of grief. And she would learn that she is not powerless but capable of will and action.

In that three-hour flight "Brenda" shifted from letting life woes define her to allowing the possibilities ahead to divine her. Her body language changed, she attempted a smile or two and as we landed we laughed at the 30,000-foot high therapy session.

She told me she had been asked to deliver a eulogy and didn't know how she was going to gather the presence of mind to do so. Yet as we walked off that plane together she told me she knew how she would begin: "I don't know why cancer claimed Sara's life and not mine. But I do know that I will live and love for both of us. It's up to me to make the difference I know Sara would have made in the world. She'll live on through me and through all of us."

~ J.P.

LESSON 17

ASK THE TOUGH QUESTIONS

"Nothing in life is to be feared. It is only to be understood."
~Marie Curie

"When you speak," Tyler Perry told Oprah, "people's lives change." Six simple words. Among all of the accolades and superlatives showered upon Oprah during her celebrated 25[tth] and final season, few words were as significant as those.

As a reporter and then talk show host Oprah was charged with two difficult tasks—keeping it interesting and entertaining without falling prey to the scandalous and using the guest's chair not to sit in judgment on an issue or choice or experience but to enlighten and educate her viewers by educating herself.

The heart of her platform was a balanced hybrid of compassion and curiosity. From that platform she could do what mentor Barbara Walter's most strongly commended her for: ask the tough questions. It's no small task sitting across from a mother who left her baby in the back seat of her car, coaxing her to relive the tragedy, requiring her to put painful memories into words. Speaking with a once physically beautiful woman whose face literally melted away in a horrific accident, asking her to contemplate what remains of inner beauty when the exterior is ravaged. Grilling former frequent guest and relationship expert Iyanla Vanzant about their seemingly acrimonious parting of ways until truth and understanding about her departure from the show connected.

Abandonment, loss, abuse, illness, pain, love, addiction. How? Why? When? With great composure, sensitivity, professionalism and warmth Oprah asked the tough questions again and again. Sometimes tears flowed. Sometimes she cut to commercial break. Every once in a blue moon she was rendered speechless, but that never stopped her from asking.

Perhaps we don't ask the questions because we think we know the answers. Perhaps we're afraid of the answers. We learned from watching Oprah that when we don't ask the tough questions we fail to get to the heart of the matter. We fail to grow closer. We fail to achieve closure. We fail to illuminate and be illuminated. We miss the crucial epiphanies that when stitched together map our soul's evolution.

> ***Asking a tough question takes guts. It also takes conviction. And when we ask the tough questions—of our friends, our families, our employees, our employers, our community and above all ourselves— lives can change.***

As a reporter I knew how to ask the tough questions. I did extensive research so my interviews could focus on intent and emotion and experience and not fact-finding. It was a delicate dance. I needed to pry to be informed but also made sure to veer away from what I deemed to be superfluous or silly gossip.

As a manager of a newspaper staff I knew how to ask the tough questions: "Your heart just doesn't seem in it. Is this really the career you want?" "Did you play hooky and spend the day on the links instead of with clients?" And even "Did you steal the money?"

As a friend I knew how to ask the tough questions: "How much longer can you endure your sister's rage without confronting her?" "Do you really think it's okay to leave your dog alone overnight while you go away for the week-end?" "Yes, that Mexico vacation would be great fun but in the long run wouldn't you be happier using that money to pay off your credit card debt instead?"

Yet as a young woman I couldn't always ask the tough questions of myself. Perhaps it's because I feared the answers. Perhaps it's because I already knew the answers and then I'd actually have to do something about my sorry state. With the tough questions buried away we can pretend to somewhat contentedly live our lives, but we can only mask our truth until that mask begins to crack.

My first marriage was a roller coaster of emotion. My ex-husband was a recovering addict whose sobriety was challenged when his father and brother died within a short time of each other. The emotional upheaval challenged his recovery. The upheaval won.

We separated for a bit but ultimately reunited through the grief and sorrow. I knew I was unhappy. I wanted a home and stability. I wanted a life filled with dreams and goals and love and joy. I wanted adventures and I wanted to make a difference. At the time he couldn't dream, he could only fight to stay sober and a home, dogs and family weren't in the cards for him. I knew this marriage wasn't my future. And yet I stayed only until I dared to ask myself the tough questions I had previously asked of others: "Are you happy?" "Is this what you want?" "Do you have the strength to leave?" Honesty gave way to divorce, which in turn paved the way for my dreams to be fulfilled.

I would love to tell you that I never fear the tough questions, but that isn't the case. Still I've learned all that "truth shall set you free" business is far from over-rated. The toughest questions, those we often recoil from, are the ones that matter most and if you want to propel your life forward or help others do the same, ask away—with compassion and without judgment. Ask away.

~ J.P.

LESSON 18

CULTIVATE FORGIVENESS

"Without forgiveness, there's no future."
~ Desmond Tutu

Some of the most powerful moments on The Oprah Winfrey Show over the years have occurred when a victim was brought face to face with a perpetrator. The perpetrator was able to express remorse and the victim was able to forgive. Time and time again Oprah brought people in conflict together and we were able to watch the emotional transformations take place in front of our eyes. We have had a front-row seat to witness the power of forgiveness and the sense of freedom that transpires when we let go of pain that we perceive has been caused by another.

Bigotry, racism and violence are learned traits, passed from one generation to another, but even the most deeply entrenched beliefs can be changed when confronted with truth and reason.

Forgiveness is about moving forward and not getting stuck in the past. We only get one chance to live each moment and it is vital that we live in the present moment, in the continuing flow of life. We have learned watching scores of guests on The Oprah Winfrey Show over the years that we must let go of shame and blame in order to be fully realized human beings. We don't have to invite those who have done us wrong to be part of our lives, but we must let go of past injuries to move on with our own life journey. The quality of our lives depends on the quality of our thoughts.

> ***Forgiveness gives us the means to let go of those things we can't control, to take back the power we have given to people or events that have caused us pain and refocus our energy on that which brings us peace and joy.***

I was sixteen when my father left, leaving behind a wife, four children, a dog, a guinea pig, a hamster, a bird, a goldfish and a mortgage. I was twenty-six when I navigated my first attempt to forgive him, in the form of a lengthy, double-spaced missive at the prodding of the therapist I enlisted to help me eradicate long-standing feelings of abandonment. My wedding day was approaching and I couldn't quite shake the "men leave" notion that was firmly imprinted on my psyche. So I gave this exercise in exorcism a try. I poured buckets of feelings into the letter. I even mailed it. I received an insipid and tidy little reply—one sentence that was so insignificant I don't recall the words. I still felt deserted.

It wasn't until I was thirty-six, two whole decades after my father's departure, that I fully comprehended that forgiveness had to happen in my heart in order for me to truly be free. It was a light bulb moment—a powerful blend of self honor, release, acceptance, sorrow and joy that delivered a powerful shift in my feeling and thinking, without the bitter aftertaste.

Forgiveness, like truth, really does set you free. Father's Day no longer carries the same sting. My first marriage didn't stick but my second is a marvelous journey of love and adventure. Trust is its cornerstone and that trust only exists because forgiveness paved its way.

I don't know who I would be today if I had held on to those feelings of abandonment. I doubt I would have attracted all of the love and abundance that is in my life now. I doubt that I would know how to love as deeply as I do. When I was able to forgive my father I *banished many fears and uncertainties and the uneasy feeling of waiting for that other shoe to drop.*

It's not always easy and it doesn't always come naturally, but true forgiveness brings us one step closer to compassion, understanding and freedom and clears away the cobwebs that prevent us from fully living.

~ J.P.

LESSON 19

FIND YOUR CALLING

"It is not in the stars to hold our destiny but in ourselves."
~William Shakespeare

One of the most important lessons Oprah has taught us and something she left us with in her final show is that everybody has a calling. Everybody is somebody. We don't have to be celebrities or have a platform as large as Oprah's to make a difference in the lives of others. Just like a ripple in a pond, the kindness we extend to others, the goodness we inspire, any help and comfort we provide to others creates a positive impact that may extend beyond our line of sight. We never know who's watching or who's listening.

We can all make a difference in the world. We are each valuable and carry with us a unique gift that only we can impart to others and to our planet Earth. We are all parts of a whole. We can all become a safe and snug harbor for each other, just as Oprah's world—her show, the causes she has championed, the books she has inspired us to read, the magazine she sends into our homes every month—has become a harbor for us. For those of us who didn't know where else to turn for therapy, guidance and spiritual comfort, we knew we could show up in front of our TV sets every afternoon and learn something genuine.

All of us have a gift or a calling and the purpose of our lives is to find out what that is. Our calling is that passion that lights us up. Oprah has said that feelings are our GPS. When we listen to our gut feelings we are hearing the voice of our inner being speaking to us. The more we trust our hearts, the more clearly we can find our way toward success. When we truly recognize our own self-worth we will no longer block our own blessings.

> *When we learn to harness our power to our passion there is no limit to what we can achieve. The sweetest satisfaction results from doing our heart's bidding.*

One of the first astrologers I'd ever met looked at my chart and told me that unlike many people who are destined to become doctors or lawyers or enter any number of professions, I had a free pass this time around, though with Mars in Virgo in the 6th House, a life of service through health and healing was indicated. I thought it ironic at the time since I was running a vegetarian health food restaurant, an occupation I had fallen into during years spent wandering the globe. Then he added, "Well, you're never going to be famous with your name in lights, but among a high-profile and special group of people you are going to be very well-known."

Flash forward a few years. I was now a single mother living in San Francisco, the sole supporter of my two-year-old daughter and attempting to put my life back together after a few serious setbacks. I awoke one morning with the gnawing feeling that I was not doing what I was supposed to be doing. My former jet-setting hippie lifestyle was no longer feasible now that I was a parent. I tried to meditate but couldn't quiet my mind, so I prayed—something I didn't often do—and asked for guidance.

I awoke the next morning and couldn't stop thinking about my friend and lover David, the most selfless and spiritual man I'd ever known. Before anyone knew what bodywork was, he had taught me about pressure point massage and healing through herbs and homeopathy. David had died the previous year in a plane crash. Yet I knew he had come and gone in my life for a reason. I decided at that moment that I would carry the torch David left behind and I would become a massage therapist. To do so I would need to find the best teacher I could find but it was 1974 and the cornucopia of healing modalities we have access to today was non-existent then.

There was one man I had met in my hometown of Phoenix a few years before, Ted, who seemed to know something about healing and bodywork. When I consulted my trusty I Ching as to whether or not he could help me, the hexagrams pointed to a resounding affirmation. Within the week I had packed up and driven home to Phoenix.

At my first meeting with Ted I told him of my decision to study massage and asked if he would train me in his methods.

"What I practice is intuition and you can't teach intuition," he told me. "I've tried to train people before but they always did more harm than good. But you're very sincere and I like you. Perhaps I could train you along with my son, but first I'd like you to study with Mary Burmeister here in Scottsdale. She spent many years studying with a master in Japan and you could learn all the basics from her."

I called Mary as soon as I could and enrolled in her class only to discover it wasn't massage at all that she was teaching but rather an ancient Japanese healing art called Jin Shin Jyutsu. As soon as she began explaining this discipline my ears pricked up. I knew in an instant that I had found what I had been seeking for so many years and I was just as certain that I would be a practicing student of Jin Shin Jyutsu for the rest of my life. I never went back to Ted except to thank him. Thirty-six years later Jin Shin Jyutsu is still my passion as well as my profession. I had been halfway around the world to find my heart's desire, my true calling, in the very place I grew up.

~ N.M.

LESSON 20

DO WHAT YOU LOVE

"Go confidently in the direction of your dreams. Live the life you've imagined."
～ Henry David Thoreau

Nearly 5,000 episodes. (4,561 to be precise). Nearly 30,000 guests. And the number of days Oprah missed work? Zero. Nada. Zilch. Not one.

Precedent says it would have been okay. After all, the king of nighttime TV, Johnny Carson, repeatedly had guest hosts throughout his thirty years on air. We would have tuned in to see Gayle or Stedman wing it for an episode or two while Oprah visited a spa or took in a fall foliage bike tour or just spent a day or two chilling with a book while occasionally glancing out at the beauty of Lake Michigan from her Chicago penthouse.

We've taken the occasional day off so why shouldn't she? Call it a tireless commitment. Call it an inability to relinquish control. Call it assuming full responsibility for a show that carried her name. But the way we see it, Oprah was doing what she loved. "You and this show have been the great love of my life," she told the audience during her final episode. Even when you're sick or tired you don't send in a pinch hitter to do the work you love. You muster up your enthusiasm, harness your gratitude, show up and do the work that fills your heart and fuels your soul.

Oprah taught us that when we do what we love the work is its own reward. She taught us that when we do what we love it's a privilege, not a weighted responsibility. And she taught us that when we do what we love we can do it with unbridled enthusiasm for a stunning twenty-five years.

> *Do what you love and you'll never work a day. Do what you love and the money will follow. Do what you love and love what you do. Taking a cue from Oprah, here's one more for that list: Do what you love, do it brilliantly and when it's time to stop doing it, say a graceful farewell. And find something new to love.*

I first dabbled in writing at the age of ten. A grade school teacher submitted a thirty-page story I wrote the previous summer to a Young Author's Conference, a formidable event at a sprawling college campus that aimed to encourage children to pursue a life and love of writing. I received an award, high praise and a perfect bound copy of my work. The fanfare was fun but the real kicker was that at an early age I found something I loved to do and was encouraged to do more of it. What a gift.

I never did write another short story. But six years later I found myself on my high school newspaper staff. As a high school junior I landed a plum job writing for the local community newspaper. Three years later I held an editor's position on the staff of a college newspaper. The pay was slim but the writing was pure joy. I did some freelance work and met and interviewed interesting people, including Jane Fonda, Carl Bernstein, Ian Hunter and Walter Cronkite. I reviewed a young Jim Carrey, scooped Barbara Walters on an exclusive interview with a visiting Russian diplomat and met my goal of having an article printed in the Detroit Free Press before graduation.

Journalism degree and Smith Corona typewriter in hand, I headed west to make my mark. I wrote for glossy magazines. I wrote for community newspapers. I wrote for dailies, weeklies and monthlies. Sometimes I wrote for free. Sometimes I wrote for barter scrip at a restaurant. Sometimes I was paid enough to put a few gallons of gas in my car. But I never gave thought to the paycheck. I was working three jobs that allowed me to cobble together enough to pay basic living ex-

penses, which in turn afforded me the freedom to write for free if need be.

I recently told a friend that a business venture could only be called a hobby if he isn't monetizing it. I was wrong. If you do what you love the rewards will come. As for my own story I found I had a head for business and ultimately helmed one of the top newsweeklies in the country. I still penned a story every now and then but for the most part, that part of me was dormant until I launched my own chain of newspapers, writing hundreds of articles each year for over five years. I churned out story after story, in the process wholly unleashing the writer within.

Today I have my own small press, nurturing authors and writing books that matter. I don't consider myself a spectacular writer. I do know my writing is authentic, it gets a point across and on occasion it moves the reader. I also know that I am doing what I love and I have never been happier.

~J.P.

LESSON 21

BE A STUDENT FOR LIFE

"Education is the most powerful weapon which you can use to change the world."
~ Nelson Mandela

Mrs. Duncan must be beaming. For twenty-five years her former 4th grade student used her daytime podium to passionately extol the virtues of learning and the lifelong pursuit of expanding one's brain and consciousness. Sometimes Oprah was the student. Sometimes she was the teacher. And we the viewers were always the beneficiaries of her hunger for knowledge. From scholars to celebrities, spiritual thinkers to politicians, Oprah had an uncanny ability to bridge entertainment and knowledge, delivering resounding lessons and encouraging us to learn more and do more.

We learned to be book smart, health smart, people smart and spiritually wise. We learned that learning is a fluid part of life and that it doesn't end with a diploma. Learning is enriching and rewarding and it is our responsibility to seek the teachers, to take the classes, to do the work.

Sometimes the learning is fun. Sometimes it's functional. Often, it's both. Sometimes it comes with ease. Sometimes it's challenging.

But it's always worthwhile.

Canine expert Tamar Geller taught Oprah how to train her golden retriever puppies. Jay Z taught Oprah to rap. Martha Stewart even taught her how to fold a fitted sheet. Yes, we learned to identify a properly fitting bra and the ideal S-shaped curve of a healthy bowel movement. We also earned about the power of teamwork, the grace of God and, according to guest Shirley MacLaine, that UFO's resemble clouds.

We learned the power of one person to make a difference. We learned that Australia is a nice place to visit with a planeful of friends. And we learned from Michelle Rhee, former chancellor of Washington D.C. schools, that teachers must be held accountable for their performance and that the future of our children depends upon dramatic education overhaul.

It's no surprise that as we go to press we learn that Oprah will be teaching at her Oprah Winfrey Leadership Academy for Girls in South Africa. Ever the teacher she will take her lesson plans to the airwaves on OWN and will continue to make good on the pledge she made to Nelson Mandela to help turn the tide of that nation.

A pledge to life long learning doesn't necessarily require a master's degree at an Ivy League school. It requires a master's degree in life. Whether we take an online class, read a book each week, engage in meaningful dialogue, attend workshops and lectures, learn a craft or learn a trade, we are laying the groundwork to amplify our life experience. In doing so we will impact the experience of those around us for we will then become the teachers ourselves.

When we strive to be a student for life we embrace knowledge, understanding and possibilities. We connect history, culture and humanity. We don't sit idly while the next generation sails by and we are better equipped to boldly navigate the world with awareness and ease.

A single sentence trumpeting my bachelor's degree in journalism from Michigan State University sits on the very bottom of my résumé. But I don't consider this acknowledgement of my formal education the main attraction. And that, I believe, illustrates one of Oprah's lessons I relate to most: be a student for life.

It would take reams of paper to document all I've learned since graduating one year after East Lansing's most famous student Magic Johnson. I've learned about politics and spirituality, culinary techniques and dance, painting, culture, archeology and landscape architecture and health and real estate and photography and finance and management and animals and technology. And that's just the tip of the iceberg.

I've learned that we are all so much more than our résumés.

I've learned there's not enough time to assimilate all of the information we'd like to in this lifetime. I've learned that the brain is indeed similar to a malleable muscle and given the appropriate attention and exercise it can be powerful when flexed.

Above all I've learned there are many ways to acquire knowledge and expand horizons. Travel, reading, workshops, lectures and community college courses are all forums in which we can continually broaden the mind.

I have this thing about learning something new every day. I don't like to let my head hit my pillow at night without having accumulated a new factoid, a new perspective or even a new word. It wasn't until I took an online course in Constitutional Law out of pure curiosity that my quest to learn expanded expo-

nentially. Poetry Writing, European Art and How to Be a Vet Technician are just some of the affordable courses I have enjoyed online.

Unlike reading or watching a documentary (both otherwise excellent learning opportunities) there is a layer of accountability if you take it seriously. Reading assignments, writing assignments, quizzes, tests and final exams are all part of the online curriculum. I can have frequent email exchange with the instructor and other students. I can "attend" class any time of day from pretty much anywhere in the world. I can wear PJs while I learn. I can have a puppy on my lap. Surprisingly I enjoy the discipline of being a student.

All that's required to be a student for life is a sense of adventure and a little bit of time every day. And an awareness that adding information and understanding to our daily existence allows us to be more present and ultimately more enriched and satisfied.

~ J.P.

LESSON 22

CREATE A VISION BOARD

"For I dipped into the future, fast as human eye could see, saw the vision of the world and all the wonder that would be."
~Alfred, Lord Tennyson

"When I grow up..." As children we dreamed wistfully about the way our adult lives would look. We spoke freely of unicorns, fairy tales and mermaids. Adults found it absolutely adorable when we puffed out our little chests and spoke unabashedly of plans to be an astronaut or even president of the United States...someday.

And yet when we are unleashed full throttle into adulthood—into "someday"—dreaming is often replaced with infinite responsibility, not infinite possibilities. Dreams are often back burnered, destined to live in a land far, far away from our day-to-day realities.

Enter the Vision Board—a practical tool that encourages dreaming and goal setting. Think of it as the crock pot conspirator. It does its job even when we are otherwise occupied.

For Ellen DeGeneres, months of calls to secure an *O Magazine* cover turned out futile. It was after she deployed a vision board that things shifted. "You have to put it out there to the universe and it will come to you," she told her audience. And yes, she did nab that O Magazine cover.

Okay, okay, I know what you're thinking. Yes Ellen does have a little more pull than we have sitting in our kitchens pouring through magazines and photos to create our own masterpiece of wishful thinking. Whether you're a wealthy talk show host or a struggling single parent there's one thing we all have access to—the power of manifestation.

For those who shy away from woo woo principles consider it an exercise in quantum thinking—the energy of thoughts attracting the energy of the action. Spiritual or scientific, it works. Assign no limitations. Dismiss preconceived notions. Embrace the possibility that in creating a blueprint for your dreams, a lovely little collage that keeps your eye on the prize, even your childhood fantasies can be a reality. After all, astronauts and presidents were once dreamers.

Creating a vision board is a bold declaration that you can have clarity about your dreams and are willing to commit to your part in their fulfillment. It's also about knowing you are worthy of these dreams being realized. Dreams aren't freebies. They are fulfilled because you do the work.

> *Assembling our goals and dreams in a tangible form allows us to be clear and focused about what we want most in our lives. The process of creating a vision board is a journey unto itself and when approached with zeal and purpose we unleash a life where dreams can truly be fulfilled.*

Sometime in the mid-90's I became friends with Mimi, a lawyer turned neuro-linguistic programmer and life coach. It was she who first introduced me to the idea of a vision board though at the time she called it a "treasure map." I was told to create this board using photos, inspiring quotes and phrases, whatever images I could conjure up and to place it somewhere where I would see it every day. The idea is that these images seep into our subconscious mind and then manifest in our conscious life. What a concept!

As a compulsive list-maker I loved the idea of this vision board. Many times in the past things I had written on my "wish lists" had turned up or had happened. This project sounded like a lot more fun. I couldn't wait to begin.

I bought construction paper, glue, glitter and other craft supplies, grabbed a huge stack of magazines and began tearing through them. I found images of the Eiffel Tower to represent Paris, my favorite city, photos of horseback riding in Ireland, a gorgeous beach on the island of Kauai, a photo of Oprah (Doesn't everyone have a picture of Oprah on their vision board for a myriad of reasons?), a photo of Ed Bradley of 60 Minutes fame. (I had a crush on him at the time.) I even pasted my face onto the body of a Victoria's Secret model.

When the call came fulfilling a long time desire of mine to travel on a world tour with a rock and roll band as their massage therapist I was jumping for joy. Our first destination was Kauai. The day I arrived I put on my swimsuit, ran down to the beach and jumped in the ocean. I looked up at the mountain at the end of the beach and got that goose-bump feeling of déjà vu. I ran back to the sand to get my camera and took a photo of the beach and the mountain from just that spot in the water where I had been standing. Months later, when I returned from the tour and developed my photos I compared the Kauai beach on my vision board to the photo I had taken—same angle, same clouds in the sky and, except for the lighting, a nearly identical photo.

As I studied the vision board I had made so many months before I realized how many of my "visions" had manifested. Met Oprah, check. Met Ed Bradley, check. Went to Paris, check. Saw horses in Ireland, check. Did my body look like the Victoria's Secret model's? Not exactly, but I did spend two months traveling all over Europe with the band, staying in five-star hotels and eating fabulous food and I still managed to lose a few pounds which was something of a miracle.

Have I recommended creating vision boards to everyone I know who is in need of a life-lift. You betcha!

~ N.M.

LESSON 23

BE OF SERVICE

"I slept and dreamt that life was joy.
I awoke and saw that life was service.
I acted and behold, service was joy."
~ Rabindranath Tagore

Oprah once tweeted, "If you operate from the paradigm of service, I know your life will have more value and you will be happy." The truth of that statement is clear. Over and over we have watched people's lives transform because they chose to give back and stand for something larger than themselves.

The greatest leaders are those who lead by example and what an example we have had in Oprah. We her viewers probably don't even know the full scope of Oprah's giving back. In fact, Oprah herself might not be aware of all the lives she has changed as evidenced by one of the most thrilling and inspiring moments to take place on her show. As part of the tribute to Oprah in the farewell spectacular at the United Center, we learned that over 400 African American young men who would not have otherwise received a college education did so because of Oprah's endowment to a Morehouse College scholarship fund. Over 300 of these men walked through the United Center, each carrying a candle, honoring the gift they had been given. And they weren't stopping there: the Morehouse men had signed a pledge to raise money for scholarships of their own because they wanted to help those who would come after them. What an unforgettable moment that was.

Inspired by the creativity of a little girl who began collecting pennies to donate to charities, Oprah started the Angel Network and inspired change of her own, helping to build schools and homes among other projects. Through the Angel Network Oprah set armies of volunteers marching.

Yet Oprah's lessons and teachings to us were never more poignant than in her show finale when she urged us not to waste any more time. "Start embracing the life that is calling you and use your life to serve the world."

Being of service and giving of our time and resources is a privilege and a joy. It means that our lives are full enough to be able to pay forward some of the blessings we've received. It means we're aware that our time and commitment have value. Sometimes it's enough to give a smile to someone you see on the street or give a compliment to the cashier who is checking your groceries, or to show up at a senior center or animal rescue just to spread some love. Being able to be of service to others and to this Earth that sustains us is why we're here.

Back in the day, whenever I had a momentous decision to make, I would consult the I Ching, a book of oracles from the collective great minds of ancient China. I remember distinctly that when I consulted the I Ching about the wisdom of opening my own health food restaurant, one phrase stuck in my mind and has remained there ever since: "If a man would rule he must first learn to serve."

I had my own fine example of service to others that I could follow, that of my mother. She seemed to be perpetually cooking for charity, whether it was her church fundraisers, pizza for the hospital fair where she volunteered as a nurses' helper or an annual dinner for 500 to raise funds for an Armenian college. After the college fundraiser Mom could hardly walk from days of preparing shish kebab, rolling stuffed grape leaves and making rice pilaf and baklava in enormous quantities. She still returned to do it again year after year. In between she brought food to anyone who was sick as well as to families who had lost loved ones. On top of that she also worked full-time, first in the family carpet business and then as a top-selling realtor. And she still found time to entertain, something she loved to do.

It's no wonder that I fell into the type of work that I did—introducing people to a healthy lifestyle in my restaurant and later as a massage therapist and acupressurist. Nothing has been more gratifying to me than helping others feel better, except perhaps teaching others how to keep themselves healthy.

Still, whenever I compared my "good works" to what others were doing around the globe I always felt inadequate. That somehow with all of the turmoil go-

ing on in the world I just wasn't doing enough. Then I would run across someone I hadn't seen in a while who would tell me that meeting me had changed the entire direction of his or her life, or that I had somehow saved or helped that individual. It was in those situations that I realized I had been doing what I was meant to be doing all along—that I had been of service after all.

As Oprah said in her final show, each of us has our own platform, whether large or small, and that is where our power lies. My mother was my first teacher who showed me the importance of being of service to others and to this life. That has been a source of power for me and it is a power I will stay connected to always.

~ N.M.

LESSON 24

NOURISH AND NURTURE YOURSELF

"Tell me what you eat and I will tell you who you are."
~ Anthelme Brillat-Savarin

When you learn something, pass it on. If there is anyone on the planet that maxim applies to it's Oprah Winfrey. Oprah first learned from fitness trainer Bob Greene to make the connection between what she was eating and what was eating her. Greene helped her accomplish this by asking the right questions, such as "What kind of life do you want to live?" And because of her connection to Greene, Oprah has helped all of us to ask the right questions of ourselves.

Oprah has admitted she's had a rocky relationship with food and had long misunderstood its role in her life. In the past she has said that food was comfort, pleasure, love, a friend and a substitute for emotions. Now she uses it in healthful moderation to nourish and sustain her body. She turned her newfound enlightenment into a lesson so that we, her viewers, could also make the connection between our emotional states and how we feed ourselves. Yes we have watched Oprah go on a few fad diets. We have watched her weight yo-yo and heard her declare herself "vegan-ish" because she still wanted to eat the eggs of the happy chickens that live next door in Montecito. We've also watched her learn that when her weight climbs it means her life is out of balance and it's time to play, relax and put herself first for a while

To further help us achieve optimum health Oprah brought Dr. Oz on board. We now know more about antioxidants than some of the experts, not to mention other normally embarrassing topics like passing gas and pooping. Male viewers even learned they could add length to their penises by losing weight. No stone has been left unturned in Oprah's quest to help people improve their lives by improving their health.

When Oprah finds something or somebody that moves her spirit or inspires her, something that tastes good or is good for people in general, she shares it and we become the beneficiaries of her largesse. Because Oprah herself has been willing to run a marathon, get proper medical tests and change her diet, she has inspired us to do the same.

> ***Nourishing our physical selves, making peace with food and relishing the sensory elements of epicurean delights in a healthy and non-destructive manner permits us to participate in community and culture without guilt or self-judgment.***

I've always wished I were twenty pounds lighter even when I was twenty pounds lighter. Weight has been an issue in my life since my first family vacation—ten days on a luxury ocean liner to and from Hawaii with seven-course breakfasts, seven-course lunches and ten-course dinners, not to mention tea time, cocktail hour and the infamous midnight buffet. I was seven years old and never questioned why anyone would want to eat at midnight when they should be sleeping. Once we landed in Hawaii I developed a passion for banana-macadamia nut pancakes, drowning in coconut syrup. I am certain I created industrial-strength fat cells at that tender age and have been plagued by them ever since. So can I relate to Oprah's diet blunders and weight fluctuations over the years? Yes I can. Have I indulged in emotional eating like Oprah did before she met Bob Greene? Yes I have.

If there was a fad diet out there it had my name on it. From drinking Sego ("See the pounds go") to eating only grapefruit and hard-boiled eggs, I tried them all. In my late teens a friend introduced me to Professor Arnold Ehret's Mucusless Diet Healing System and overnight I went from the Standard American Diet to becoming a strict vegetarian. I read books by all the health fanatics. I became a fanatic myself and attempted to convert everyone I knew, first opening a health food restaurant and later writing and teaching healthy cooking classes. Then, like Oprah, I discovered exercise.

Living in Los Angeles in the 80's I was able to feel the burn with Jane Fonda herself. Aerobics became the order of the day and I took the plunge. I bartered mas-

sages for exercise classes with some of L.A.'s top fitness instructors and by the time I hit my forties I was in enviable shape, but I had gone from one extreme to the other. As a Buddhist I worried that I was spending too much time shaping a body that was impermanent.

These days I have found a comfortable balance. It's still hard to think of myself as a senior, although I don't mind the discounts. I still indulge in pancakes on occasion but they are the whole wheat variety with pure maple syrup. I manage a modicum of daily exercise I enjoy, mainly hiking and walking. I'm healthy and happy and I still wish I were twenty pounds lighter.

~ N.M.

LESSON 25

ENDINGS AREN'T ENDINGS; THEY'RE BEGINNINGS IN DIFFERENT SUITS OF CLOTHING

"There's a trick to the 'graceful exit.' It begins with the vision to recognize when a job, a life stage or a relationship is over and let it go. It means leaving what's over without denying its validity or its past importance to our lives. It involves a sense of future, a belief that every exit line is an entry; that we are moving up rather than out."
~ Ellen Goodman

The Chicago studio that Oprah called home was a swell of emotion the day of the final installment of *The Oprah Winfrey Show*. It was a candid and compelling hour of gratitude and reflection, sprinkled with laughter and tears. On the heels of the hoopla that surrounded her final season it was a modest farewell but in its simplicity it packed a powerful punch. With her magazine and OWN network and no doubt many other tricks up her sleeve, Oprah will have an abundance of opportunities to continue to share, teach, inspire, engage and entertain. But for that hour, with the world watching, she took to the airwaves with her own version of *The Last Lecture*.

True to form Oprah didn't use the last show to parade her remarkable achievements. Instead, the final hour was a selfless offering of parting thoughts. Words to live by. Thoughts to ponder. A love fest for her viewers. Gratitude for their loyalty. Above all it was a nod to the extraordinary tale of a poor little Black girl from rural Mississippi who arguably is now the most famous and influential woman in America if not the world.

It was not a bittersweet goodbye for Oprah. Her joy was palpable. She had planned on leaving five years earlier but her Earth angel Mattie Stepanek told her she wasn't done then, it wasn't time to leave—that twenty-five was her number.

The most extraordinary moment of that final show might have been overlooked if you blinked an eye or dabbed a tear away. It came after Oprah said her goodbye to her audience, after she walked the halls passing her formidable team of producers and staff. The last lesson appeared when she scooped her dog Sadie into her arms with a joyous glee reserved for freedom and completion and unbridled enthusiasm for what awaits.

What's this? Unlike the tears Dorothy wept when she said farewell to her Yellow Brick Road companions, our last images of Oprah on May 25, 2011 were nothing short of high-octane joy. It wasn't a painful goodbye. It was a giddy hello.

What a lesson. Yes, farewells can be heart wrenching, but in these final moments, Oprah, ever the teacher, showed us the glee in goodbye. That farewell is really a "hello" in a different suit of clothing.

Love, energy, time, life—It's all fluid. Goodbye isn't final. It's not an ending. It's transformational. It's a beginning. "We did it, Sadie," she said.

Indeed she did.

The LA Weekly was a scrappy and hip alternative Los Angeles newspaper a mere five years old when I was hired as an assistant in the advertising department. Typewriters, not computers, sat on our desks. Newspapers were raging in popularity and nothing had its finger on the pulse of the thriving Los Angeles metropolis like the Weekly. It was a thrilling time for a journalist in her early twenties looking to make her mark in the world. Funny how sometimes it's the world that makes its mark on us.

I was a bit of an innocent at the time and my learning curve was high. I encountered people with piercings and tattoos, men and women who were formerly homeless, former addicts, single mothers struggling to make ends meet alongside would-be actors and artists. I also met brilliant thinkers and great manipulators, stand-up comics and spiritual teachers. Over the years, Midwest sensibility and work ethic tethered to my soul, I was promoted again and again. Eighteen years later I was named publisher of the now formidable media company.

On September 10, 2001 I decided that I had done all I could do with the company I was so good to and that was so good to me. I knew I had other work to do. I wrestled with how to tell my devoted staff who had worked tirelessly and joyfully with me for so many years. I was up all night struggling to find the right words. But instead of the clarity I sought what I received the next morning was a numbing dose of perspective—9/11. My decision to leave a job was hardly the cataclysmic event I'd imagined it to be the night before. I didn't even mention my imminent departure *for a few weeks. Instead I did the work that needed to be done. We had a sister publication, the Village Voice in New York City, and our friends there were rattled to their core. We all were.*

When I finally did make the announcement there were some tears, there was some sadness, but above all there was support. They knew what I knew. They knew what Oprah knows. Endings aren't finite. They are about closing one door so we can open another. And they are essential to the core of our human experience. Graceful endings pave the way to extraordinary beginnings. It has been ten years since I left the place I called home for nearly twenty and the memories still delight, the friendships endure and the lessons permeate all I do.

~ J.P.

ACKNOWLEDGEMENTS

Thanks to Joel, Thomas, Daniel and Hutch for your enthusiasm for this book.

Thanks to Rachel Heller for your fetching copyediting skills.

And to the masterfully talented Hugh Syme for your friendship and creative genius.

Thanks to Eddie Michaels for your tireless support.

Special thanks to Spencer, for being you and for being there. Always and all ways.

Thanks to Coco, Michele, Margo, Karen, Kelly, Jeannie, Robin, Gwen, Debbie, Mari, Joi, Alison, Bridget, Jennifer, Sterling, Morgan, Patrick, Jessica, Jody Blue and Vedra for your encouraging words and perspective.

And to a lifetime of teachers, including Oprah, thank you for showing us the way.

www.ingramcontent.com/pod-product-compliance
Lightning Source LLC
Chambersburg PA
CBHW032140040426
42449CB00005B/329